Coffee Shop Discussions
The Foundations of "Good" Discussion

英語で発信力を鍛えるディスカッション
―日常トピックスで考えを伝えてみよう！―

Alan Bossaer

NAN'UN-DO

Coffee Shop Discussions
The Foundations of "Good" Discussion

英語で発信力を鍛えるディスカッション
―日常トピックスで考えを伝えてみよう！―

Copyright © 2019
by
Alan Bossaer

All Rights Reserved.
No part of this book may be reproduced in any form without written permission from the author and Nan'un-do Co., Ltd.

このテキストの音声を無料で視聴（ストリーミング）・ダウンロードできます。自習用音声としてご活用ください。
以下のサイトにアクセスしてテキスト番号で検索してください。

https://nanun-do.com　テキスト番号 [**511999**]

※ 無線 LAN（WiFi）に接続してのご利用を推奨いたします。

※ 音声ダウンロードは Zip ファイルでの提供になります。お使いの機器によっては別途ソフトウェア（アプリケーション）の導入が必要となります。

※ Coffee Shop Discussions の音声ダウンロードページは以下の QR コードからもご利用になれます。

To the Students

Welcome to ***Coffee Shop Discussions***! This book was written for any student (High Beginner/Intermediate/Advanced) who wants to express their opinions in English but who lacks confidence in their vocabulary or language skills and/or would like to learn, how to have a good discussion.

One of the first things you will discover about a discussion class is that it is different from a conversation class. Much more vocabulary is needed, critical thinking skills are vital, and there is more structure. In this book you will learn the skills of discussion, new vocabulary, and how to use your knowledge of the topic and your critical thinking skills in order to present your opinions clearly and logically.

Coffee Shop Discussions has many examples of *new language* for you to use, but it also allows you to use the English you have already learned. The discussion topics in this book are topics that most of you will be familiar with which will make it easier for you to form an opinion. In fact, most of you will already have opinions on the topics. This book has been designed to give you the tools necessary to express those opinions.

At first, having a discussion in English will feel strange (and challenging) but after a few units, you will understand the structure of a discussion and become more and more comfortable and confident. Many students have trouble discussing a topic (logically) for one minute in English. By the time you finish this course, many of you will be able to carry on a discussion for 8 to 10 minutes.

Happy discussing!

Contents

Unit 1	Welcome to Coffee Shop Discussions!	5
Unit 2	Western-style Hotel vs Japanese Inn - Part 1	10
Unit 3	Western-style Hotel vs Japanese Inn - Part 2	14
Unit 4	e-Learning - Part 1	18
Unit 5	e-Learning - Part 2	22
Unit 6	Clubs and Circles - Part 1	26
Unit 7	Clubs and Circles - Part 2	30
Unit 8	Social Networking - Part 1	34
Unit 9	Social Networking - Part 2	38
Unit 10	Big City vs Small Town - Part 1	42
Unit 11	Big City vs Small Town - Part 2	46
Unit 12	Online Shopping - Part 1	50
Unit 13	Online Shopping - Part 2	54
Unit 14	Students Working Part-Time - Part 1	58
Unit 15	Students Working Part-Time - Part 2	62

Unit 1: Welcome to Coffee Shop Discussions!

A Let's Get Started!

Read the two dialogs below. Which dialog do you think is a **discussion**? Which one is just a **conversation**? Why?

Dialog _____ is a discussion because it has _____.

Dialog 1

A: **So**, what did you do yesterday?
B: **Oh**, I just stayed at home and watched TV. How about you?
A: Me? **Ah**, I went shopping with my mom.
B: What did you buy?
A: **Umm**, I bought a hat and some shoes.
B: Nice.

Dialog 2

A: **So**, what do you think about the new school uniforms?
B: Me? **Umm**, I like them. They're so comfortable.
A: Really? I disagree. I think they're uncomfortable. I mean, they don't feel good.
B: **Hmm**, yeah, maybe, but …

B The First Step in a Discussion – Giving an Opinion

We now know that discussions often have opinions. In the cartoon bubbles below, underline the opinions. How many opinions are there?

There are _____ opinion(s).

I really think Tokyo Disneyland is much better than Universal Studios!

I disagree. Universal Studios is better than Tokyo Disneyland.

Giving an opinion is the first step in a discussion.

People can agree and/or disagree with an opinion because it is (not) a fact.

Fact: Tokyo is a big city.
          [You can't disagree.]
Opinion: Tokyo is the best city in Japan.
          (Someone might disagree)

5

Unit 1

Pairwork **Groupwork**

With a partner or in a small group, practice giving your opinion on the topics below. If you agree with your partner or classmates, express agreement. If you disagree, show disagreement.

1. Getting married at 20
2. Online shopping
3. A game center on campus
4. K-Pop vs J-Pop
5. Horror movies and comedies
6. Smartphones for junior high school students

Stating (giving) opinions
- "I think getting married at 20 is okay / not a good idea."
- "I really think horror movies are better than comedies."
- "I think tea is better than coffee."

Expressing agreement
- "I agree."
- "That's true."
- "You're right."

Expressing disagreement
- "I disagree."
- "Umm, I don't agree."
- "Umm, I think ___ is/are better."

C The Second Step in a Discussion – Pros and Cons (support)

Giving an opinion is an important step in a discussion. It usually comes at the beginning of the discussion or near the beginning. However, we also need support or reasons to help make our opinion stronger. The support part of the discussion is where we give good and bad points. We often call these good points "pros or benefits" and we call the bad points "cons or drawbacks." Having many good points (pros) and bad points (cons) makes our opinion stronger.

What are two other ways to say **pros**? What are two other ways to say **cons**? Write them below.

Pros = _____ Cons = _____

_____ _____

Pairwork   Groupwork

With a partner or in a small group, think of two or three pros and cons for a game center on a university campus.

A game center on campus

Pros (good points)

1. _____
2. _____
3. _____

Cons (bad points)

1. _____
2. _____
3. _____
4. _____

D The Third Step in a Discussion – Building Vocabulary

Opinions and support are key elements of every good discussion. However, it is important to build up a strong vocabulary as well. Without vocabulary, it is difficult to have a meaningful discussion.

> SHHH...
> This game center is noisy!

Example #1 -
Weak vocabulary and weak or no support

A: I think a game center on campus is not good.
B: Really? Why?
A: Umm, it's bad.
B: I think so, too.

This discussion has an opinion but it doesn't have support. The word **bad** is very simple and is just repeating the opinion in different words. We don't know why a game center is not good (i.e. bad).

Example #2 - Stronger vocabulary with stronger support

A: I think a game center on campus is a bad idea.
B: Really? Why?
A: Umm, it's **distracting**. I mean, students <u>can't focus on their studies</u>.
B: Hmm, but a game center could be **refreshing**. I mean, it <u>could relieve their stress</u>.

> This discussion has opinions and stronger support. The word **distracting** is a stronger word than **bad**. Student A also gives a simple meaning of the word **distracting** (i.e. "can't focus on their studies") which makes the word **distracting** clear. Student B disagrees and also gives strong support with the word **refreshing** and the meaning (i.e. "could relieve their stress").

E The Fourth Step in a Discussion - Disagreeing

2

In Part B, we learned that there are different ways to disagree with someone's opinion. Listen to the four dialogs below. Fill in the missing disagreement words.

Dialog# 1

A: I love our new school uniform. It's so stylish. What do you think?
B: Really? _____. I think the design is too simple.

Dialog# 2

A: Social networking sites are risky. I mean, they can be dangerous.
B: _____. I think social networking is safe.

Dialog# 3

A: I think an iPad is more convenient than a laptop. I mean, it's easier to carry.
B: _____ a laptop has more storage.

Dialog# 4

A: An iPad is lighter than a laptop.
B: _____, but many laptops are light, too. And they have more memory than an iPad.

F One More Important Point about This Textbook – Q & A

In this book, students ask and answer many questions related to the topic. By asking questions, students get a deeper understanding of a topic. It's also a good way to learn new vocabulary and grammar you can use in your discussions.

Pairwork **Groupwork**

1. Here are some questions that are related to the topic of a game center on campus. In pairs or in small groups, ask and answer the questions below.

   Q1: What do you think is the main purpose of going to university?

   Q2: What's a good way to make new friends on campus?

   Q3: What's a good way for university students to relieve stress?

   Q4: Are there places on campus where students can relax?

   Q5: Do you think students can stay focused on their studies if there is a game center on campus?

2. Here is a list of Pros and Cons for a game center on campus. The pros and cons are connected to the questions above. Decide which sentences are pros and which are cons. Write the letter in the correct column. Fill in any blanks using the questions and/or your own ideas. Is your idea a pro or a con?

Game Center on Campus – Pros and Cons

Pros (Benefits)
1. _____
2. _____
3. _____
4. _____

Cons (Drawbacks)
1. _____
2. _____
3. _____
4. _____

A. A game center on campus is a good place to make _____.

B. A game center is too noisy.

C. A game center is fun so it's good for relieving stress.

D. I think university students will lose focus on studying if there is a game center on campus.

E. Some students may forget the main purpose of going to university.

F. School is difficult and students need a place to _____ _____.

G. (your idea) _____
_____.

Unit 2

Western-style Hotel vs Japanese Inn Part 1

A **Preview** **Pairwork** Check (✓) the information about yourself. Then, have a conversation with a partner by changing the statements into questions and asking each other the questions.

___ I have stayed at an expensive western-style hotel.

___ I have stayed at a Japanese inn (*ryokan*).

___ I often enjoy spending time in quiet, peaceful, remote places.

___ I would rather sleep **in** a bed than **on** a *futon*.

___ I love being outdoors in nature.

___ I have been to many *onsens*.

___ Shopping is my favorite leisure activity.

___ I enjoy taking pictures of scenic places.

B Listening 3

1. Check (✓) the information you hear.

   Betty wants to stay at a western-style luxury hotel because ...

   ☐ she thinks western-style hotels have many amenities.
   ☐ she wants to swim in a pool.
   ☐ she likes shopping a lot.

   Frank wants to stay at a Japanese inn because ...

   ☐ he thinks Japanese inns have many amenities.
   ☐ he likes soaking in an *onsen*.
   ☐ he likes traditional Japanese food.

2. Listen again.
   Circle (○) the amenities you hear. 4

   Amenities
   pool   gyms   kitchen
   in-house restaurants and bars
   80 inch TV   room service

C **Building Support – Q & A** `Pairwork` Get a partner. Ask and answer the questions in the box. Give a reason or reasons for your answers.

Example: *"I think a western-style luxury hotel / a Japanese inn has better amenities. For example, it has …*

1. Which has better amenities—a western-style luxury hotel or a Japanese inn?
2. Which has better traditional Japanese food—a western-style luxury hotel or a Japanese inn?
3. Which is more scenic—a western-style luxury hotel downtown or a Japanese inn in the mountains?
4. Which is more relaxing—a western-style luxury hotel or a Japanese inn?

D **Pros / Cons** Make a list of Pros (Good Points) and Cons (Bad Points) for staying at a western-style luxury hotel downtown and for staying at a Japanese inn in the countryside. Use information and language you learned from pages 10 and 11 and your own ideas and language.

western-style luxury hotels

Pros (Good Points)	Cons (Bad Points)
	They are usually very expensive.

Japanese inns

Pros (Good Points)	Cons (Bad Points)
They have great traditional Japanese food.	

Unit 2

E **Vocabulary** Choose the correct adjective to match its definition (meaning). Write it in the space. Add *two of your own* adjectives. *Add the meanings of the two new adjectives.*

convenient	boring	uncomfortable	relaxing	_____
quaint	noisy	luxurious	pricey	_____

1. A western-style hotel can be ___*pricey*___. I mean, it can be expensive.
2. A Japanese inn in the countryside is _____. I mean, it's refreshing.
3. Many western-style hotels are _____. I mean, they are very comfortable.
4. A Japanese inn in the countryside is _____. I mean, there's not much to do.
5. A western-style hotel downtown is _____. I mean, it's not so quiet.
6. Many Japanese inns are _____. I mean, they are very charming.
7. A western-style hotel downtown is _____. I mean, it is in a handy location.
8. Many Japanese inns are _____. I mean, they don't feel good.
9. Many western-style hotels are _____.
   I mean, _____.
10. Many Japanese inns are _____.
    I mean, _____.

F **Vocabulary – Expanded** Circle (◯) the word or expression in each group that is *not* directly connected to the meaning of the adjective (in red or in blue).

Group 1	luxurious	lavish	(quiet)	comfy
Group 2	noisy	busy	loud	not peaceful
Group 3	uncomfortable	not relaxing	inconvenient	unpleasant
Group 4	relaxing	refreshing	necessary	calm
Group 5	convenient	friendly	in a suitable area	easily accessible
Group 6	boring	dull	helpful	not exciting
Group 7	quaint	old-fashioned	traditional	large
Group 8	pricey	expensive	costly	attractive

G Speaking – Expressing Disagreement

Scenario: Two people are discussing their 3-day trip to Kyoto. One person wants to stay at a luxurious western-style hotel in the city and the other person wants to stay at a Japanese inn outside the city (i.e. in the countryside).

Dialog 1 Pairwork In pairs, practice the dialogs. Decide who is A and B. Use the cues in the box. For each adjective you must give the meaning! When finished, change roles!

A quaint / relaxing   B boring / uncomfortable

A: Do you think we should stay at a hotel in the city or at a Japanese inn in the countryside?
B: Hmm, I think a Japanese inn in the countryside is better.
A: Really? How come?
B: Well, many Japanese inns are _____.
   Pro (adjective)
A: What do you mean?
B: I mean, _____.
   (Meaning)
A: Yeah, maybe, but I think a Japanese inn in the countryside is _____.
   Con (adjective)
B: _____? Why do you say that?
   (repeat adjective)
A: Well, _____.
   (Meaning)

Dialog 2 Pairwork Practice the dialogs. Give the adjective AND the Meaning! When finished, change roles!

A luxurious / convenient   B pricey / noisy

A: Do you think we should stay at a western-style hotel in the city or at a Japanese inn in the countryside?
B: Hmm, I think a western-style hotel in the city is better.
A: Really? How come?
B: Well, many western-style hotels are _____.
   Pro (adjective)
A: What do you mean?
B: I mean, _____.
   (Meaning)
A: Well, yeah, maybe, but I think a western-style hotel is _____.
   Con (adjective)
   I mean, _____.
   (Meaning)

Unit 3

Western-style Hotel vs Japanese Inn — Part 2

A Building Support

Finish the sentences with language from the purple box.

1. Many Japanese inns are quaint. I mean, they are very charming
   because _g_ .

2. Many western-style hotels are luxurious. I mean, they are very comfortable
   because ____ .

3. A Japanese inn in the countryside is relaxing. I mean, it's refreshing
   because ____ .

4. A western-style hotel downtown is convenient. I mean, it is in a handy location
   because ____ .

5. A Japanese inn in the countryside is boring. I mean, there's not much to do
   because ____ .

6. A western-style hotel downtown is noisy. I mean, it's not so quiet
   because ____ .

7. Many Japanese inns are uncomfortable. I mean, they don't feel good
   because ____ .

8. A western-style hotel downtown can be pricey. I mean, it can be expensive
   because ____ .

---

a) it's near many shops and restaurants. And, it's easy to get to

b) it has an *onsen* and it's surrounded by nature. It's also very quiet and peaceful

c) they have many amenities, spacious rooms, and big, comfortable beds

d) it's located downtown. And, they are usually big so they have a lot of staff to pay

e) it's in a remote area, far from shops and restaurants. And, it has few amenities or attractions

f) there are a lot of people staying at the hotel. There are also a lot of city noises

g) they have traditional Japanese food and simple, traditional Japanese-style rooms

h) they don't have a bed. And, you have to sit on the floor

B Building Support – Q & A `Pairwork` `Groupwork`

With a partner or in a small group, ask and answer the questions.

1. What kind of fun things can you do in a luxurious western-style hotel?
2. What is an example of traditional Japanese food?
3. Would you pay 100,000 yen a night for a hotel room?
4. What kind of noises can you hear in a hotel downtown?
5. What does a traditional room in a Japanese inn look like?
6. What are some different ways you can get to a hotel downtown?

C Support in Context and Disagreeing

1. Listen to the dialog. Fill in the blanks with the words you hear.

A: Do you think we should stay at a western-style hotel downtown, or a Japanese inn in the countryside?

B: I think we should stay at a western-style hotel downtown.

A: Really? How come?

B: Well, many western-style hotels are **luxurious**. I mean, they are very comfortable because they _____ many amenities. They also _____ spacious rooms, and big, comfortable beds.

A: Yeah, some western-style hotels are **luxurious**, but they are also **pricey**. I mean, they _____ pretty expensive. A hotel downtown _____ cost more than 50,000 yen a night.

B: Well, they _____ **pricey** but a western-style hotel downtown is **convenient**. I mean, it is _____ a handy location. For example, it's _____ many shops and restaurants.

A: Hmm, okay. You win. Let's stay at a western-style hotel.

2. We often repeat an adjective when we disagree. The adjective "luxurious" is repeated. What other adjective is repeated? Circle (○) it.

Unit 3

D Controlled Practice Pairwork

Student A looks at this page. Student B looks at page 17. Spend a few minutes filling in the correct adjectives in the blue boxes. Take turns giving opinions about a Japanese inn and a western-style hotel. Each time you choose an adjective from the box, cross (／) it off. Try a few rounds using only blue parts. Then try a few rounds using blue + red parts. To prepare, write only key words (NOT sentences) in the red boxes before you try the dialog.

convenient	pricey	quaint	boring
relaxing	noisy	uncomfortable	luxurious

Dialog 1

Student A A starts the conversation. Choose the correct adjective to fit the dialog.

Support

1. I think we should stay at a Japanese inn in the countryside.
3. Well, a Japanese inn in the countryside is _____. I mean, it's refreshing because
5. Yeah, but many Japanese inns are _____. I mean, they are very charming because

Dialog 2

Student A Listen to Student B and choose the correct adjective to fit the dialog.

Support

2. Really? How come?
4. Yeah, but a western-style hotel downtown is _____. I mean, it's not very quiet because
6. Yeah, that's true but a western-style hotel downtown can be _____. I mean, it can be expensive because

D Controlled Practice Pairwork

Student B looks at this page. Student A looks at page 16. Spend a few minutes filling in the correct adjectives in the blue boxes. Take turns giving opinions about a Japanese inn and a western-style hotel. Each time you choose an adjective from the box, cross (/) it off. Try a few rounds using only blue parts. Then try a few rounds using blue + red parts. To prepare, write only key words (NOT sentences) in the red boxes before you try the dialog.

convenient	pricey	quaint	boring
relaxing	noisy	uncomfortable	luxurious

Dialog 1

Student B Listen to Student A and choose the correct adjective to fit the dialog.

Support

2. Really? How come?

4. But, many Japanese inns are _____. I mean, they don't feel good because

6. Yeah, that's true, but a Japanese inn in the countryside is _____. I mean, there are not many fun things to do because

Dialog 2

Student B B starts the conversation. Choose the correct adjective to fit the dialog.

Support

1. I think we should stay at a western-style hotel downtown.

3. Well, a western-style hotel downtown is _____. I mean, it's in a handy location because

5. Yeah, a western-style hotel downtown can be noisy but many western-style hotels are _____. I mean, they are very comfortable because

Unit 4: e-Learning

A Preview — Pairwork

1. Read the statements. Check (✓) the information about yourself.

Me   My Classmate

____ ____ I like studying at my own ¹**pace**.

____ ____ I like to ask the teacher questions when I don't understand something.

____ ____ I learn better by myself.

____ ____ I am good at using a computer.

____ ____ I learn best in the evening.

____ ____ I like the teacher to correct my mistakes when I study English.

____ ____ I like talking to people face-to-face when I study English.

____ ____ I get ²**frustrated** when the teacher goes too fast.

____ ____ I lose focus when I study by myself.

¹ pace = speed   ² frustrated = slightly angry

2. Change each statement above into a question and interview a classmate. Check (✓) the information about your classmate.

Examples:

Statement: I like studying at my own pace.

Question: Do you like studying at your own pace?

Statement: I like to ask the teacher questions when I don't understand something.

Question: Do you like to ask the teacher questions when you don't understand something?

e-Learning Part 1

B **Listening** Listen to the discussion and check (✓) the information you hear. 6

Rob thinks e-Learning could be good for him because …

☐ he learns better by himself.
☐ he learns best in the evening.
☐ he likes studying at his own pace.

Rob thinks a traditional classroom is better for Sophie because …

☐ she likes to ask the teacher questions when she doesn't understand something.
☐ she likes the teacher to correct her mistakes.
☐ she loses focus when she studies by herself.

C **Pros / Cons** **Pairwork** With the same partner from your Part A interview, decide if e-Learning *could be* good for your classmate. If e-Learning could be good, write **2 or 3** reasons (Pros) based on your interview on page 18. If you think e-Learning is not good for your partner, give **2 or 3** reasons (Cons) based on your interview on page 18. Give your opinion to your partner using the Pro or Con dialogs below. When done, find out what other pairs think.

Note: We use *could be* when we think something is possible, but we're not 100% sure.

Pros

A: I think e-Learning **could be** good for you.
B: Do you think so?
A: Well, ¹you _____. ²And you _____. ³And, you _____.

Cons

A: I think e-Learning is not good for you.
B: Why do you say that?
A: Well, ¹you _____. ²And you _____. ³And, you _____.

D Vocabulary
Choose the correct adjective to match its definition (meaning). Write it in the space. Add *two of your own* adjectives. *Add the meanings of the two new adjectives.*

distracting	frustrating	impersonal	flexible	_____
boring	cost-effective	efficient	stimulating	_____

1. I think e-Learning is __efficient__. I mean, it could be helpful for some people.
2. I think e-Learning might be _____. I mean, it might not be interesting.
3. I think e-Learning could be _____. I mean, it could be interesting.
4. I think e-Learning could be _____. I mean, it could be annoying.
5. I think e-Learning is _____. I mean, you can study whenever and wherever you want.
6. I think e-Learning is _____. I mean, it's a bit cold.
7. I think e-Learning is _____. I mean, it's fairly cheap.
8. I think e-Learning could be _____. I mean, it's easy to lose focus.
9. I think e-Learning could be _____.
   I mean, _____.
10. I think e-Learning could be _____.
    I mean, _____.

E Vocabulary – Expanded
Circle (○) the word or expression in each group that is not directly connected to the meaning of the adjective (in red or in blue).

Group 1	distracting	lose focus	(unsafe)	lose concentration
Group 2	frustrating	get angry easily	useful	annoying
Group 3	stimulating	interesting	exciting	dull
Group 4	efficient	useless	useful	effective
Group 5	flexible	easy to change	friendly	convenient
Group 6	cost-effective	inexpensive	educational	cost-saving
Group 7	impersonal	amazing	not interactive	remote
Group 8	boring	uninteresting	not fun	wasteful

Speaking – Discussing the Pros of e-Learning `Pairwork`

Practice the conversation with a partner. Student A chooses a Pro Adjective from the box and gives the meaning. Change roles and practice with a new adjective giving the meaning.

Pro Adjectives

flexible   stimulating
efficient   cost-effective

— Language Key —
Red Words are hesitation markers. Use them when you need a little time to think before speaking.
Blue words are words you can use to show disagreement.
Underlined words are the meanings of the adjectives.

A: What do you think about e-Learning? I mean, do you think it's good?
B: Hmm, I'm not sure. What do you think?
A: Umm, I think it has some good points.
B: Really? Like what?
A: Well, *for instance, it's flexible. I mean, you can study whenever and wherever you want.
B: Hmm, that's a good point, but it also has some drawbacks.

* for instance = for example

 Speaking – Discussing the Cons of e-Learning `Pairwork`

Practice the conversation with a partner. Student A chooses a Con Adjective from the box and gives the meaning. Change roles and practice with a new adjective giving the meaning.

Con Adjectives

distracting   frustrating
boring   impersonal

— Language Key —
Red Words are hesitation markers. Use them when you need a little time to think before speaking.
Blue words are words you can use to show disagreement.
Underlined words are the meanings of the adjectives.

A: What do you think about e-Learning? I mean, do you think it's good?
B: Hmm, I'm not sure. What do you think?
A: Umm, I think it has some *drawbacks.
B: Really? Such as?
A: Well, for one thing, I think it could be boring. I mean, it might not be interesting.
B: Hmm, that's a good point, but it also has some good points.

* drawbacks = bad points

Unit 5

e-Learning

Part 2

A **Building Support – Q & A** `Pairwork` `Groupwork`
With a partner or in a small group, brainstorm reasons for each question. Write your reasons. Finally, write the adjective that matches the Q&A. The first one has been done for you.

| boring | efficient | distracting | stimulating |
| cost-effective | frustrating | impersonal | flexible |

Matching Adjective

1. Q: Why do you think it's easy to lose focus when you study online?

   A: Umm, because _____   *distracting*

2. Q: Why do you think studying online is cheaper than studying in a classroom?

   A: Umm, because _____

3. Q: Why is studying whenever and wherever you like good for some people?

   A: Well, _____

4. Q: Why do you think e-Learning is helpful for some people?

   A: Umm, because _____

5. Q: Why do you think e-Learning could be interesting?

   A: Umm, because _____

6. Q: Why do you think e-Learning might not be interesting?

   A: Umm, because _____

7. Q: Why do you think e-Learning could be annoying?

   A: Umm, because _____

8. Q: What do you mean e-Learning is a bit cold?

   A: Well, _____

e-Learning Part 2

B Adding Support to the Adjective and Meaning

Match the **Adjective** with its **Meaning** and **Supporting** parts. Check your answers with a partner. Number ☐1 has been done for you.

Note: Some of the **Adjectives** have **more than one** **Supporting** parts!

Adjective	Meaning	Support	
I think e-Learning could be boring.	I mean, it is fairly cheap. ☐1	You can study at your own pace. ☐	You can watch a video as many times as you want. ☐
I think e-Learning is efficient. ☐2	I mean, it could be interesting. ☐	For example, sometimes your computer freezes or crashes. ☐	There's no face-to-face interaction with the teacher and other students. ☐1,
I think e-Learning could be stimulating. ☐3	I mean, it could be helpful for some people. ☐	You can study in the evening at home or in a coffee shop. ☐	You can't ask questions easily if you have a problem. ☐
I think e-Learning could be frustrating. ☐4	I mean, it's easy to lose focus. ☐	You just do the same thing again and again on the computer. ☐1,	It's easy to access your SNS or play video games online. ☐
I think e-Learning is flexible. ☐5	I mean, it might not be interesting. ☐1	You just study on a machine. ☐1,	You don't have to pay transportation costs. ☐
I think e-Learning is impersonal. ☐6	I mean, it's a bit cold. ☐	It's cheap because there is no teacher or building. ☐	You can study English with students from other countries. ☐
I think e-Learning is cost-effective. ☐7	I mean, you can study whenever and wherever you want. ☐		
I think e-Learning can be distracting. ☐8	I mean, it could be annoying. ☐		

C Support in Context and Language to Disagree 🎧7

Listen to the dialog. Fill in the blanks with the words you hear.

A: I think e-Learning has some good points.

B: Really? _____?

A: Well, _____, I think it's **stimulating**. I mean, it could be interesting. You can study using interesting videos and study with _____.

B: Yeah, but e-Learning is **impersonal**. I mean, it's a bit cold. It's just you and a machine.

A: I think it could be a bit **impersonal**, but I also think e-Learning is very **efficient**. I mean, you can study at your own pace. And, you can watch a video _____ as you want.

B: Hmm, I think we're both right.

Unit 5

D Controlled Practice Pairwork

Student A looks at this page. Student B looks at page 25. Spend a few minutes filling in the correct adjectives in the blue boxes. Take turns giving opinions about e-Learning. Each time you choose an adjective from the box, cross (∕) it off.

Try a few rounds using only blue parts. Then try a few rounds using blue + red parts. To prepare, write only key words (NOT sentences) in the red boxes before you try the dialog.

efficient	boring	stimulating	frustrating
flexible	impersonal	cost-effective	distracting

Dialog 1

Student A A starts the conversation. Choose the correct adjective to fit the dialog.

Support

1. I think e-Learning has some good points.
3. Well, for instance, e-Learning is _____. I mean, it could be helpful for some people.
5. I disagree, I think e-Learning could be _____. I mean, it could be interesting because
7. Hmm, I think we're both right.

Dialog 2

Student A Listen to Student B and choose the correct adjective to fit the dialog.

Support

2. Really? Such as?
4. Well, it could be frustrating, but e-Learning is great because it's _____. I mean, you can do it whenever and wherever you want.
6. Yeah, it could be distracting, but it's also _____. I mean, it's fairly cheap because

D Controlled Practice   Pairwork

Student B looks at this page. Student A looks at page 24. Spend a few minutes filling in the correct adjectives in the blue boxes. Take turns giving opinions about e-Learning. Each time you choose an adjective from the box, cross (✓) it off.

Try a few rounds using only blue parts. Then try a few rounds using blue + red parts. To prepare, write only key words (NOT sentences) in the red boxes before you try the dialog.

efficient	boring	stimulating	frustrating
flexible	impersonal	cost-effective	distracting

Dialog 1

Student B Listen to Student A and choose the correct adjective to fit the dialog.

Support

2. Really? Like what?
4. Yeah, but e-Learning could be _____. I mean, it might not be interesting because
6. Yeah, maybe, but e-Learning is _____. I mean, it's a bit cold.

Dialog 2

Student B B starts the conversation. Choose the correct adjective to fit the dialog.

Support

1. I think e-Learning has many drawbacks.
3. Well, e-Learning could be _____. I mean, it could be really annoying because
5. Yeah, it's flexible, but e-Learning is also _____. I mean, it's easy to lose focus because
7. Hmm, I think we're both right.

Unit 6: Clubs and Circles Part 1

A **Pros / Cons** `Pairwork` `Groupwork` What do you think about school clubs and circles? Discuss this topic for **15 – 20** minutes with a partner or in a small group. Think about good points and bad points of clubs and circles. After your discussion, write some of the important points below.

Pros – Some good points about clubs and circles
Do Later! See the bottom of page 29. ↓

1. They can make you feel refreshed. — healthy
2. _____
3. _____
4. _____
5. _____
6. _____

Cons – Some bad points about clubs and circles

1. You might not study.
2. _____
3. _____
4. _____
5. _____
6. _____

B **Listening** Listen to the discussion between Kevin and Marina. Fill in the missing words and check (✓) the information you hear.

Kevin: Hey, Marina, are you in a club or circle?

Marina: No, I'm not in a club or a circle.

Kevin: Really? _____?

Marina: Umm, I'm too shy. And, ☐ I don't have the time.
☐ I think clubs and circles are expensive.
☐ I'm not really interested in clubs or circles.

Kevin: That's too bad.

Marina: Are you in a club or circle?

Kevin: Yeah, I'm in the ☐ Ballroom Dance Club.
☐ Chess Club.
☐ French Club.

Marina: Really? How _____ have you been in the club?

Kevin: Umm, about ☐ 3 months.
☐ 6 months.
☐ 3 years.

C Interview **Groupwork**

In a small group, ask each other about your **current** club or circle experience.

Are you in a club or circle?
(If "No" ask "*Why not?*")
Which club(s) / circle(s) are you in?
How long have you been in the _____ Club?

Unit 6

D **Vocabulary** Choose the correct adjective to match its definition (meaning). Write it in the space. Add *two of your own* adjectives. *Add the meanings of the two new adjectives.*

| costly | rewarding | tiring | enjoyable | _____ |
| distracting | social | cliquey | healthy | _____ |

1. I think clubs and circles can be ___*cliquey*___. I mean, it's hard to fit in sometimes.
2. I think clubs and circles can be _____. I mean, they can be good for your mind and body.
3. I think clubs and circles can be _____. I mean, they can be a lot of fun.
4. I think clubs and circles can be _____. I mean, they can be useful.
5. I think clubs and circles can be _____. I mean, they can be exhausting.
6. I think clubs and circles can be _____. I mean, they are interactive.
7. I think clubs and circles can be _____. I mean, you might lose focus.
8. I think clubs and circles can be _____. I mean, they can be expensive.
9. I think clubs and circles can be _____.

   I mean, _____.

10. I think clubs and circles can be _____.

    I mean, _____.

E **Vocabulary – Expanded** Circle (○) the word or expression in each group that is not directly connected to the meaning of the adjective (in red or in blue).

Group 1	costly	high-priced	pricey	(luxurious)
Group 2	rewarding	beneficial	powerful	helpful
Group 3	enjoyable	time-consuming	entertaining	fun
Group 4	cliquey	exclusive	selective	convenient
Group 5	social	connecting	quaint	uniting
Group 6	tiring	helpful	exhausting	strenuous
Group 7	healthy	refreshing	amazing	relaxing
Group 8	distracting	not pay attention	noisy	get side-tracked

28

F Speaking – Expressing Disagreement `Pairwork`

Practice the conversation with a partner. Decide who is Pro and who is Con. Substitute the Pro Adjectives and the Con Adjectives. Start the conversations using different words from the yellow box. When done, try without your book (look at the adjectives your teacher has written on the board).

Pro Adjectives
- healthy
- rewarding
- social
- enjoyable

Con Adjectives
- cliquey
- tiring
- distracting
- costly

A: I think school clubs and circles are great!

great!   terrible!
fantastic!   bad!
wonderful!   awful!

B: Really? Why do you say that?

A: Well, I think they can be _____.
(Adjective)

B: Do you think so?

A: Yeah, I mean, _____.
(Meaning)

B: Hmm, yeah, maybe, but I think clubs and circles can be _____.
(Adjective)

A: _____? What do you mean?
(Repeat Adjective)

B: I mean, _____.
(Meaning)

Connecting the New Vocabulary with the Pros and Cons

Go back to page 26 where you wrote your Pros and Cons for clubs and circles. Do any of your Pros or Cons match any of the new words (i.e. cliquey, tiring, etc.)? If "Yes", write the adjective in the yellow box on page 26. For example, the example, "they can make you feel refreshed", matches the word "healthy" from our list of new words.

Unit 7 Clubs and Circles

Part 2

A Building Support – Quiz! `Pairwork` `Groupwork`
Read the statements and circle T or F or NS. Then, compare your answers with a partner or in a small group. Be prepared to give reasons and/or to give examples!

Why? For example

I see you were in the French Club at your university.

T = True / F = False / NS = Not Sure

1.	Clubs and circles can be good for job hunting.	T / F / NS
2.	You can learn different kinds of skills in a club or circle.	T / F / NS
3.	Fifteen hours a week doing club or circle activities is too much.	T / F / NS
4.	Some clubs and circles can be a bit expensive.	T / F / NS
5.	Clubs and circles can be good for your mind and your body.	T / F / NS
6.	Some students focus too much on their clubs and circles.	T / F / NS
7.	Sometimes it's hard to join a club or circle.	T / F / NS
8.	A club or circle might be good if you are a shy person.	T / F / NS
9.	University life is stressful.	T / F / NS
10.	Circles and clubs are often tiring.	T / F / NS

B Adding Support to the Adjective and Meaning

Match the Adjective with its Meaning and Supporting parts. Check your answers with a partner. Number 1 has been done for you.

Note: Some of the Adjectives have **more than one** Supporting part!

Adjective / Meaning / Support

Adjective	Meaning
I think clubs and circles can be rewarding. [1]	I mean, they can be expensive. [ ]
I think clubs and circles can be tiring. [2]	I mean, they can be useful. [1]
I think clubs and circles can be costly. [3]	I mean, they are interactive. [ ]
I think clubs and circles can be enjoyable. [4]	I mean, they can be exhausting. [ ]
I think clubs and circles can be distracting. [5]	I mean, it's hard to fit in sometimes. [ ]
I think clubs and circles can be cliquey. [6]	I mean, they can be good for your mind and your body. [ ]
I think clubs and circles can be social. [7]	I mean, they can be a lot of fun. [ ]
I think clubs and circles can be healthy. [8]	I mean, you might lose focus. [ ]

Support:

- You can do things with other people, so it's a good way to make new friends. [1,]
- You can relieve your stress when you are in a club or circle. [1,]
- For example, you can learn new skills. I learned how to give presentations in the E.S.S. club. [1]
- In my circle we often went on fun trips together. [ ]
- You might not study hard enough or do your homework. [ ]
- You can also put your club or circle experience on your résumé. [1]
- For example, if you are a shy or quiet person it might be hard to fit in. [ ]
- Some clubs and circles meet more than 15 hours a week. [ ]
- In some clubs and circles you have to buy equipment, costumes or uniforms. [ ]
- And, you often have to pay for parties and trips with your club members. [ ]
- In sports clubs you do everything together as a team. [ ]
- Playing sports or even dancing in a club or circle can make your body and mind refreshed. [1,]

C Support in Context – "I learned how to …." 🔊 9

Listen to the dialog. Fill in the blanks with the words you hear.

A: Hey, Becky, you should think about joining a club or circle.

B: Really? Why?

A: Well, for one thing, clubs and circles can be **rewarding**. I mean, they can be useful. For example, you can learn new skills. I learned _____ in my cooking circle. And in my English speaking club, I learned _____ in English. Oh, and in the brass band club, I learned _____.

D Controlled Practice Pairwork

Student A looks at this page. Student B looks at page 33. Spend a few minutes filling in the correct adjectives in the blue boxes. Take turns giving opinions about clubs and circles. Each time you choose an adjective from the box, cross (✓) it off.

Try a few rounds using only blue parts. Then try a few rounds using blue + red parts. To prepare, write only key words (NOT sentences) in the red boxes before you try the dialog.

costly	rewarding	tiring	enjoyable
distracting	social	cliquey	healthy

Dialog 1

Student A A starts the conversation. Choose the correct adjective to fit the dialog.

Support

1. I really think you should join a club or circle.
3. Well, for one thing, clubs and circles can be _____. I mean, they can be useful.
5. Well, some clubs and circles can be tiring, but clubs and circles can be _____. I mean, they can be a lot of fun.
7. Hmm, ... you have some good points.

Dialog 2

Student A Listen to Student B and choose the correct adjective to fit the dialog.

Support

2. Really? Why?
4. Yeah, but, I think clubs and circles can be _____. I mean, you might lose focus.
6. Yeah, maybe, but clubs and circles are also _____. I mean, it's hard to fit in sometimes.
8. You have some good points, too. Maybe I'll think about it.

D Controlled Practice Pairwork

Student B looks at this page. Student A looks at page 32. Spend a few minutes filling in the correct adjectives in the blue boxes. Take turns giving opinions about clubs and circles. Each time you choose an adjective from the box, cross (/) it off.

Try a few rounds using only blue parts. Then try a few rounds using blue + red parts. To prepare, write only key words (NOT sentences) in the red boxes before you try the dialog.

| costly | rewarding | tiring | enjoyable |
| distracting | social | cliquey | healthy |

Dialog 1

Student B Listen to Student A and choose the correct adjective to fit the dialog.

Support

2. Really? Why?
4. Yeah, but clubs and circles can be _____. I mean, they can be exhausting because
6. Yeah, maybe, but clubs and circles can also be _____. I mean, they can be expensive.
8. You have some good points, too. Maybe I'll think about it.

Dialog 2

Student B B starts the conversation. Choose the correct adjective to fit the dialog.

Support

1. I think clubs and circles are great!
3. Well, clubs and circles can be _____. I mean, they can be good for your mind and body.
5. Hmm, that's possible, but I think clubs and circles are _____. I mean, they are interactive.
7. Hmm, … you have some good points.

Unit 8 Social Networking

Part 1

A Pros / Cons Pairwork Groupwork What do you think about social networking? Discuss this topic for 15 – 20 minutes with a partner or in a small group. Think about good points and bad points of social networking. After your discussion, write some of the important points below.

Pros – Some good points about social networking
Do Later! See the bottom of page 37.

1. You can use it easily. — convenient
2. _____
3. _____
4. _____
5. _____
6. _____

Cons – Some bad points about social networking

1. You might do it too much.
2. _____
3. _____
4. _____
5. _____
6. _____

Social Networking Part 1

B Listening

 10

1. Listen to the discussion and check (✓) the information you hear.

   Alice feels social networking is awful because …
   - ☐ it's too much.
   - ☐ it's unsafe.
   - ☐ it's stressful.

   Kevin thinks social networking is wonderful because …
   - ☐ it's informative.
   - ☐ he can keep in touch with his family.
   - ☐ there are many fun things you can do.

2. Listen to the discussion between Noah and Becky. Fill in the missing words. 11

   Noah: So, Becky, which social networking _____ do you use?

   Becky: Umm, I use Facebook, Instagram and Line.

   Noah: Which _____ do you use the most?

   Becky: Oh, I probably use Instagram the most because I really love sharing photos with my friends. How about you, which social networking _____ do you use?

   Noah: I don't use any social networking sites because I think _____ waste of time. I have to study.

C Interview `Pairwork`

Ask your partner about the SNS they use.

A: "Which social networking sites do you use?"
B: "I use LINE, Facebook and Twitter. I probably use _____ the most because … ."
B: "I don't use any social networking sites because … ."

35

Unit 8

D **Vocabulary** Choose the correct adjective to match its definition (meaning). Write it in the space. Add **two of your own** adjectives. **Add the meanings of the two new adjectives.**

addictive	informative	superficial	enjoyable	_____
risky	vital	convenient	overwhelming	_____

1. I think social networking is _addictive_. I mean, many people can't stop doing it.
2. I think social networking can be _____. I mean, it's a bit shallow.
3. I think social networking is _____. I mean, there are many fun things you can do.
4. I think social networking is _____. I mean, we really need it.
5. I think social networking is _____. I mean, you can use it easily.
6. I think social networking sites are _____. I mean, you can get a lot of useful information.
7. I think social networking can be _____. I mean, sometimes it can be unsafe.
8. I think social networking can be _____. I mean, it can be stressful.
9. I think social networking is _____.

    I mean, _____.

10. I think social networking is _____.

    I mean, _____.

E **Vocabulary – Expanded** Circle (◯) the word or expression in each group that is not directly connected to the meaning of the adjective (in red or in blue).

Group 1	risky	dangerous	unsafe	(exhausting)
Group 2	overwhelming	stressful	powerful	too much
Group 3	enjoyable	time-consuming	entertaining	fun
Group 4	vital	important	necessary	useless
Group 5	convenient	useful	friendly	handy
Group 6	informative	helpful	educational	tiring
Group 7	addictive	can't stop	amazing	constantly using
Group 8	superficial	phony	shallow	wasteful

Speaking – Expressing Disagreement   `Pairwork`

Practice the conversation with a partner. Decide who is Pro and who is Con. Substitute the Pro Adjectives and the Con Adjectives. Start the conversations using different words from the yellow box. When done, try without your book.

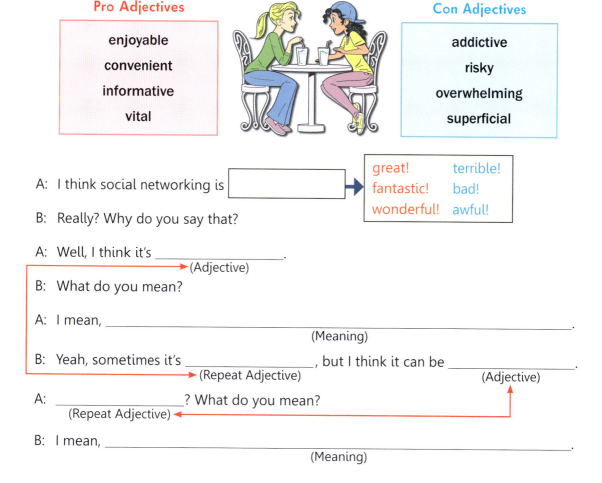

A: I think social networking is _____ → great! / terrible! / fantastic! / bad! / wonderful! / awful!

B: Really? Why do you say that?

A: Well, I think it's _____.
(Adjective)

B: What do you mean?

A: I mean, _____.
(Meaning)

B: Yeah, sometimes it's _____, but I think it can be _____.
(Repeat Adjective)   (Adjective)

A: _____? What do you mean?
(Repeat Adjective)

B: I mean, _____.
(Meaning)

Connecting the New Vocabulary with the Pros and Cons

Go back to page 34 where you wrote your Pros and Cons for SNS. Do any of your Pros or Cons match any of the new words (i.e. addictive, vital, etc.)? If "Yes", write the adjective in the yellow box on page 34. For example, the example, "You can use it easily", matches the word "convenient" from our list of new words.

Unit 9 Social Networking Part 2

A **Building Support – Q & A** `Groupwork`

Write questions that match the answers. Ask and answer the questions in groups of 3 or 4. Can you ask follow-up questions? Look at the question word hints below for help. Finally, write the adjective that matches the Q&A. The first one has been done for you.

risky	addictive	superficial	overwhelming
vital	enjoyable	convenient	informative

Matching Adjective

1. Q: Have you ever received a strange message or photo on a social networking site?
   A: Yes, I have received a strange message or photo on a social networking site.   *risky*

2. Q: _____?
   A: Umm, yes, I need social networking.

3. Q: _____?
   A: Well, for example, on SNS, I get information about my favorite artist and the latest trends.

4. Q: _____?
   A: Well, I think social networking is convenient because I can do it anytime and anywhere.

5. Q: _____?
   A: Yeah, sometimes social networking can be stressful.

6. Q: _____?
   A: Yes, I think social networking is a bit shallow.

7. Q: _____?
   A: Umm, I check my SNS at least two or three times an hour.

8. Q: _____?
   A: Umm, well, for example, I look at photos on Instagram and follow my favorite music artist on Twitter.

Have you ever ...?   What kind of ...?   What other kind of ...?
Why ...?   How many times a day ...?   How often ...?   Do you think ...?
When do you ...?   What do you do on ...?   Where do you ...?

38

Social Networking Part 2

B Adding Support to the Adjective and Meaning

Match the **Adjective** with its **Meaning** and **Supporting** parts. Check your answers with a partner. Number 1 has been done for you.

Note: Some of the **Adjectives** have **two** **Supporting** parts!

Adjective	Meaning	Support	
I think social networking can be risky.	I mean, it can be stressful. [ ]	For example, you can do it on the train or bus—anywhere. [ ]	Sometimes I have to spend 3 or 4 hours responding to my friends' posts. It's too much! [ ]
I think social networking can be overwhelming. [2]	I mean, you can get a lot of useful information. [ ]	For example, someone could steal your private information. [1]	For example, many people just post selfies and talk about themselves. [ ]
I think social networking is enjoyable. [3]	I mean, many people can't stop doing it. [ ]	For example, I need it to keep in touch with my family and friends. [ ]	You can get information about the latest trends and even world news. [ ]
I think social networking is vital. [4]	I mean, there are many fun things you can do. [ ]	For example, you can chat with your friends and share photos. [ ]	Some people have to constantly check their SNS. [ ]
I think social networking is convenient. [5]	I mean, it's a bit shallow. [ ]	For example, you can get information about restaurants and good stores. [ ]	Some people have fake profiles and you can't trust them. [1]
I think social networking is informative. [6]	I mean, we really need it. [ ]	My best friend is always on his SNS until late at night. He can't stop. [ ]	It's fun to watch videos on YouTube. [ ]
I think social networking is addictive. [7]	I mean, sometimes it can be unsafe. [1]		
I think social networking can be superficial. [8]	I mean, you can use it easily. [ ]		

C Support in Context and Language to Disagree 🔊 12

Listen to the dialog. Fill in the blanks with the words you hear.

A: I think social networking is _____!

B: Really? How come?

A: Umm, I really think social networking is **informative**. I mean, you can _____ a lot of useful information. _____, I often _____ information about the latest fashion.

B: Yeah, but social networking is so **superficial**. I mean, it's a bit shallow. For example, a lot of people just post selfies and talk about _____.

A: I think it _____ **superficial**, but I really think social networking is **vital**. I mean, we really need it. For example, I need it to _____ with my friends and my parents.

Unit 9

D Controlled Practice Pairwork

Student A looks at this page. Student B looks at page 41. Spend a few minutes filling in the correct adjectives in the blue boxes. Take turns giving opinions about social networking. Each time you choose an adjective from the box, cross (╱) it off.
Try a few rounds using only blue parts. Then try a few rounds using blue + red parts. To prepare, write only key words (NOT sentences) in the red boxes before you try the dialog.

convenient	informative	addictive	risky
overwhelming	superficial	vital	enjoyable

Dialog 1

Student A A starts the conversation. Choose the correct adjective to fit the dialog.

Support

1. I think social networking is great!
3. Well, social networking is _____. I mean, there are _____ fun things you can do.
5. Yeah, sometimes that's true, but social networking is _____. I mean, we really need it.

Dialog 2

Student A Listen to Student B and choose the correct adjective to fit the dialog.

Support

2. Really? How come?
4. I agree, it can be informative, but social networking can be _____. I mean, _____ can be stressful.
6. Yeah, sometimes it's convenient, but it's also _____. I mean, many people can't _____ doing it.

D Controlled Practice Pairwork

Student B looks at this page. Student A looks at page 40. Spend a few minutes filling in the correct adjectives in the blue boxes. Take turns giving opinions about social networking. Each time you choose an adjective from the box, cross (✓) it off.
Try a few rounds using only blue parts. Then try a few rounds using blue + red parts. To prepare, write only key words (NOT sentences) in the red boxes before you try the dialog.

| convenient | informative | addictive | risky |
| overwhelming | superficial | vital | enjoyable |

Dialog 1

Student B Listen to Student A and choose the correct adjective to fit the dialog.

Support

2. Really? Why do you say that?
4. Yeah, but social networking can be _____. I mean, sometimes it _____ be unsafe.
6. Yeah, maybe, but social networking is _____. I mean, it's _____ bit shallow.

Dialog 2

Student B B starts the conversation. Choose the correct adjective to fit the dialog.

Support

1. I think social networking is wonderful.
3. Well, social networking sites are _____. I mean, you can _____ a lot of useful information.
5. Yeah, it can be overwhelming, but social networking is _____. I mean, _____ can use it easily.

Unit 10: Big City vs Small Town

Part 1

A — Q & A Pairwork
Get a partner. Ask and answer the questions using time expressions from the orange box. Ask follow-up questions.

Questions with **How often**?

Example:
A: How often do you go downtown?
B: Umm, I rarely go downtown.
A: Really? Why not?
B: It's too crowded.

Q1: **How often** do you take public transportation?
Q2: **How often** do you eat out with friends?
Q3: **How often** do you go to concerts?
Q4: **How often** do you go shopping for clothes?
Q5: **How often** do you go to the hospital or clinic?
Q6: **How often** do you go to sporting events?

> Umm, I _____ all the time.
> Umm, I _____ quite often.
> Umm, I _____ sometimes.
> Umm, I rarely _____.
> Umm, I never _____.
> Umm, not so often.

B — Listening

1. Listen to Barbara and Alex talking about living in a big city and a small town. *13*

   Alex likes living in a small town because …
   - [ ] he thinks small towns are quaint.
   - [ ] he doesn't like pollution.
   - [ ] people talk to their neighbors.

   Barbara likes living in a big city because …
   - [ ] she thinks big cities are convenient.
   - [ ] she thinks big cities have more things to do.
   - [ ] she likes eating out a lot.

2. Listen again. Check (✓) the activities Barbara likes to do. *14*

   Barbara likes …
   - [ ] going to baseball games
   - [ ] going to museums
   - [ ] eating out
   - [ ] going to malls
   - [ ] going to concerts

42

C **Pros / Cons** Make a list of Pros (Good Points) and Cons (Bad Points) for living and working in a big city or a small town. Use information and language you learned from page 42 and your own ideas and language.

Big city

Pros (Good Points)	Cons (Bad Points)
	They can be very expensive.

Small town

Pros (Good Points)	Cons (Bad Points)
The people are friendly.	

Unit 10

D **Vocabulary** Choose the correct adjective to match its definition (meaning). Write it in the space. Add *two of your own* adjectives. *Add the meanings of the two new adjectives.*

| convenient | dull | costly | healthy | _____ |
| neighborly | inconvenient | exciting | nerve-racking | _____ |

1. Big cities can be ___costly___. I mean, they can be expensive.
2. Small towns are _____. I mean, they're boring.
3. Big cities can be _____. I mean, they can be stressful.
4. Small towns are _____. I mean, they are good for your mind and body.
5. Big cities are _____. I mean, they have everything you need.
6. Small towns are _____. I mean, people are friendly.
7. Big cities are _____. I mean, there are many interesting things to do.
8. Small towns are _____. I mean, they don't have many conveniences.
9. Big cities are _____.
   I mean, _____.
10. Small towns are _____.
    I mean, _____.

E **Vocabulary – Expanded** Circle (○) the word or expression in each group that is not directly connected to the meaning of the adjective (in red or in blue).

Group 1	convenient	helpful	(cliquey)	useful
Group 2	dull	loud	boring	uninteresting
Group 3	healthy	refreshing	efficient	good for you
Group 4	costly	expensive	necessary	pricey
Group 5	inconvenient	unfriendly	not useful	not handy
Group 6	exciting	fun	helpful	interesting
Group 7	neighborly	friendly	sociable	vital
Group 8	nerve-racking	hectic	tense	luxurious

44

F Speaking – Expressing Disagreement Pairwork

In pairs, practice the dialogs. Decide who is A and B. Choose an adjective and give the correct meaning!

A: Would you rather live in a big city or a small town?

B: A big city, of course.

A: Really? How come?

B: Well, big cities are ___*convenient / exciting*___.

   I mean, _____.
   (Meaning)

   How about you? Would you rather live in a big city or a small town?

A: Me? Oh, I would rather live in a small town.

B: Really? Why?

A: Well, small towns are ___*neighborly / healthy*___.

   I mean, _____.
   (Meaning)

B: Well, yeah, some are, but small towns are ___*dull / inconvenient*___.

   I mean, _____.
   (Meaning)

A: Yeah, maybe, but big cities are ___*nerve-racking / costly*___.

   I mean, _____.
   (Meaning)

Unit 11: Big City vs Small Town — Part 2

A Building Support – "has" and "have" Pairwork

Circle (◯) **has** or **have** and fill in all the blank spaces. Compare your answers with a partner.

A big city is **convenient**. I mean, it has everything you need.	A big city [(has) / have]	good public transportation. For example, it [(has) / have] many trains, buses, and taxis. And they run many times _____ the day.
	It also [has / have]	good **health care**. A big city [has / have] many _____ and clinics. It also [has / have] many specialists. And, there are also many drugstores.
	And, big cities also [has / have]	shopping malls so you can get everything you need in _____ place.
	And, in a big city,	shops, stores and many other places are open late.
	And, big cities [has / have]	many companies, restaurants and shops so there are many job opportunities.
Big cities are also **exciting**. I mean, there are many interesting things to do.	Big cities [has / have] Add your own answers! ➡	many entertainment places. For example, you can go to a _____, or a _____ or to a _____.
	They also [has / have] Add your own answers! ➡	_____ _____ which are enjoyable.
A big city can be **nerve-racking**. I mean, it can be stressful.	A big city [has / have]	_____ jams.
	And, in a big city,	it is crazy at rush _____ on the trains and subway.
	And, big cities [has / have]	many cars, buses and taxis, so driving can be really tense. It's also noisy.
Big cities are also **costly**. I mean, they can be expensive.	In a big city,	the cost of living is high. For example, the price of food is high. house and land prices are high. the cost of services is high. apartment rent is high.

B Building Support – "has / have / doesn't have / don't have / is / are" — Pairwork

Circle (○) **has** or **have** or **doesn't have** or **don't have** and **is** or **are** and fill in all the blank spaces. Compare your answers with a partner.

Small towns are **healthy**. I mean, they can be good for the mind and body.	Small towns [has / (have)]	fresh, clean air.
	They also [has / have]	fresh, delicious _____.
	And, small towns [is / are / have / has]	**scenic**. I mean, they are often surrounded by beautiful nature.
	And, a small town [is / are / have / has]	less stressful. The pace of life is slower than a big city.
Small towns are also **neighborly**. I mean, people are very friendly.	In a small town	everybody knows everybody.
	And, in small towns	people often help each other.
	And, small towns [has / have]	many town events and festivals. Everybody often helps or participates.
A small town is **inconvenient**. I mean, it doesn't have many conveniences.	A small town [don't have / doesn't have]	good, public _____.
	And, it [don't have / doesn't have]	many hospitals or clinics. *Add your own answers!* ⬇
	And, it [don't have / doesn't have]	many _____ _____.
	And, in a small town	shops and restaurants often _____ early.
Small towns are **dull**. I mean, they are boring.	Small towns [don't have / doesn't have]	many entertainment places.
	And, in a small town there is nothing to do. *Add your own answers!* ➡	For example, you can't go to a museum or art gallery, or go _____ _____.
		And, you can't go to a _____ _____.
		You also can't go to _____ _____.

Unit 11

C Controlled Practice Pairwork

Student A looks at this page. Student B looks at page 49. Spend a few minutes filling in the correct adjectives in the blue boxes. Take turns giving opinions about big city and small town. Each time you choose an adjective from the box, cross (/) it off.

Try a few rounds using only blue parts. Then try a few rounds using blue + red parts. To prepare, write only key words (NOT sentences) in the red boxes before you try the dialog.

convenient	dull	costly	healthy
neighborly	inconvenient	exciting	nerve-racking

Dialog 1

Student A A starts the conversation. Choose the correct adjective to fit the dialog.

Support

1. Would you rather live in a big city or a small town?
3. Really? How come?
5. Yeah, but small towns are _____. I mean, they're boring.
7. But, a small town is _____. I mean, it doesn't have many conveniences.

Dialog 2

Student A Listen to Student B and choose the correct adjective to fit the dialog.

Support

2. I think I'd rather live in a big city.
4. Well, big cities are _____. I mean, they have everything you need.
6. Yeah, but a big city is _____. I mean, there are many interesting things to do.
8. Hmm, you're right about some things, but I still like big cities.

C Controlled Practice Pairwork

Student B looks at this page. Student A looks at page 48. Spend a few minutes filling in the correct adjectives in the blue boxes. Take turns giving opinions about big city and small town. Each time you choose an adjective from the box, cross (/) it off.
Try a few rounds using only blue parts. Then try a few rounds using blue + red parts. To prepare, write only key words (NOT sentences) in the red boxes before you try the dialog.

| convenient | dull | costly | healthy |
| neighborly | inconvenient | exciting | nerve-racking |

Dialog 1

Student B Listen to Student A and choose the correct adjective to fit the dialog.

Support

2. I think I'd rather live in a small town.
4. Well, small towns are _____. I mean, they are good for your mind and body.
6. Yeah, maybe, but small towns are _____. I mean, people are friendly.
8. Hmm, you're right about some things, but I still like small towns.

Dialog 2

Student B B starts the conversation. Choose the correct adjective to fit the dialog.

Support

1. Would you rather live in a big city or a small town?
3. Really? How come?
5. Yeah, that's true, but big cities can be _____. I mean, they can be stressful.
7. Hmm, but big cities are _____. I mean, they can be expensive.

49

Unit 12 — Online Shopping

A   Pros / Cons `Pairwork` `Groupwork` What do you think about online shopping? Discuss this topic for **15 – 20** minutes with a partner or in a small group. Think about good points and bad points of online shopping. After your discussion, write some of the important points below.

Pros – Some good points about online shopping
Do Later! See the bottom of page 53. ↓

1. You can read product reviews. — practical
2. _____
3. _____
4. _____
5. _____
6. _____

Cons – Some bad points about online shopping

1. You often have to use a credit card.
2. _____
3. _____
4. _____
5. _____
6. _____

B Listening

 15

1. Listen to the discussion and check (✓) the information you hear.

   Janet feels online shopping is not good because ...
   - ☐ it's a waste of time.
   - ☐ you might shop too much.
   - ☐ it can be unreliable sometimes.

   Tim thinks online shopping is good because ...
   - ☐ it's easy to find what you want.
   - ☐ it saves him time.
   - ☐ you can do it anytime and anywhere.

2. Listen to the discussion between Jonah and Frieda. Fill in the missing words. 16

Jonah: So, Frieda, have you ever _____ anything online?

Frieda: Umm, yeah, lots of times.

Jonah: What kind of things _____ you buy online?

Frieda: Umm, I often _____ clothes. And, sometimes I _____ cosmetics. And once, I _____ a drone. How about you? Have you ever bought anything online?

Jonah: Umm, no, I haven't. I think shopping online can be distracting. I mean, I might not get anything _____. And, I don't want to use my credit card because I don't want to put my personal information online.

C Interview Groupwork

In a small group, ask each other about your online shopping experience.

→ Have you ever bought anything online?
(If "No" ask "Why not?")

What kind of things do you buy online?
"I often/sometimes buy ... ."

Have you bought anything interesting or unusual?
"Once, I bought ... ."

Unit 12

D **Vocabulary** Choose the correct adjective to match its definition (meaning). Write it in the space. Add *two of your own* adjectives. Add the meanings of the two new adjectives.

| unsafe | unreliable | time-saving | relaxing | _____ |
| troublesome | practical | economical | time-consuming | _____ |

1. I think online shopping is __time-consuming__. I mean, you might spend too much time doing it.
2. I think online shopping can be _____. I mean, you can't always trust online shopping.
3. I think online shopping is _____. I mean, it's very useful.
4. I think online shopping can be _____. I mean, sometimes it's a *hassle.
5. I think online shopping is _____. I mean, you can shop comfortably.
6. I think online shopping is _____. I mean, you can save money.
7. I think online shopping can be _____. I mean, sometimes it can be dangerous.
8. I think online shopping can be _____. I mean, it can save you time.
9. I think online shopping is _____.
   I mean, _____.
10. I think online shopping is _____.
    I mean, _____.

* hassle = a problem

E **Vocabulary – Expanded** Circle (◯) the word or expression in each group that is not directly connected to the meaning of the adjective (in red or in blue).

Group 1	unsafe	dangerous	(vital)	not secure
Group 2	unreliable	stressful	not dependable	untrustworthy
Group 3	time-saving	time-consuming	quick	decreases time
Group 4	practical	helpful	beneficial	useless
Group 5	relaxing	comfy	friendly	easy to do
Group 6	economical	cost-saving	educational	cost-effective
Group 7	time-consuming	long	lengthy	comfy
Group 8	troublesome	a problem	bothersome	addictive

Online Shopping Part 1

F Speaking – Expressing Disagreement `Pairwork`

Practice the conversation with a partner. Decide who is Pro and who is Con. Substitute the Pro Adjectives and the Con Adjectives. Start the conversations using different words from the yellow box. When done, try without your book.

Pro Adjectives
- economical
- practical
- relaxing
- time-saving

Con Adjectives
- unreliable
- unsafe
- time-consuming
- troublesome

Start words:
- great!   terrible!
- fantastic!   bad!
- wonderful!   awful!

A: I think online shopping is [fantastic!]

B: Really? Why do you say that?

A: Well, I think it's _____.
   (Adjective)

B: What do you mean?

A: I mean, _____.
   (Meaning)

B: Yeah, sometimes it's _____, but I think it can be _____.
   (Repeat Adjective)   (Adjective)

A: _____? What do you mean?
   (Repeat Adjective)

B: I mean, _____.
   (Meaning)

Connecting the New Vocabulary with the Pros and Cons

Go back to page 50 where you wrote your Pros and Cons for online shopping. Do any of your Pros or Cons match any of the new words (i.e. unreliable, practical, etc.)? If "Yes", write the adjective in the yellow box on page 50. For example, the example, "You can read product reviews", matches the word "practical" from our list of new words.

Unit 13: Online Shopping

Part 2

A Building Support – Q & A   Groupwork

Write questions that match the answers. Ask and answer the questions in groups of 3 or 4. Can you ask follow-up questions? Look at the question word hints below for help. Finally, write the adjective that matches the Q&A. The first one has been done for you.

| unsafe | time-saving | troublesome | economical | _____ | Can you think of other adjectives? |
| unreliable | time-consuming | practical | relaxing | _____ | |

Matching Adjective

1. Q: Have you ever had a problem buying something online with a credit card?
   A: Umm, yeah, once I had a problem buying something online with a credit card.   unsafe

2. Q: Do you _____?
   A: Yeah, I think shopping online is quick.

3. Q: _____?
   A: Yes, I have had to go to the post office to return a product I bought online.

4. Q: _____?
   A: Yes, I think products online are cheaper than in a store.

5. Q: _____?
   A: Umm, no, online shopping is not always reliable.

6. Q: _____?
   A: Yes, sometimes I spend way too much time shopping online.

7. Q: _____?
   A: Yes, I think online shopping is more comfortable than shopping in person.

8. Q: _____?
   A: Yes, I think most online shopping sites are helpful.

> Have you ever ...?   What happened?   What kind of problem?
> Why ...?   Why did you have to return the product?   Why not?

Online Shopping Part 2

B Adding Support to the Adjective and Meaning

Match the Adjective with its Meaning and Supporting parts. Check your answers with a partner. Number 1 has been done for you.

Note: Some of the Adjectives have **two** Supporting parts!

Adjective	Meaning	Support	
I think online shopping can be unsafe. [1]	I mean, you can't always trust online shopping. [ ]	You can't see or touch the product. Sometimes it's the wrong size or color. [ ]	You can't talk to a clerk if you have questions. [ ]
I think online shopping can be unreliable. [2]	I mean, sometimes it's a hassle. [ ]	Someone could steal your credit card information. And, some sites are fake. [1,]	Some sites have fake brands and the quality is poor. [1,]
I think online shopping can be time-saving. [3]	I mean, you can save money. [ ]	You don't have to pay transportation costs. And, there are no clerks or building. [ ]	It might take a long time for shipping. [ ]
I think online shopping can be troublesome. [4]	I mean, it can save you a lot of time. [ ]		
I think online shopping can be time-consuming. [5]	I mean, you can shop comfortably. [ ]	Shopping online is fun. Some people do it for hours and hours. [ ]	You can do it on your smartphone or on an iPad. [ ]
I think online shopping is economical. [6]	I mean, it's very useful. [ ]	If you get the wrong product or item, you have to send it back yourself. [ ]	You can read product reviews and also compare products and prices. [ ]
I think online shopping is practical. [7]	I mean, sometimes it can be dangerous. [1]		
I think online shopping is relaxing. [8]	I mean, you might spend too much time doing it. [ ]	You can do it in a few minutes. You just have to click the mouse. [ ]	You don't have to spend time going to the store. [ ]

C Support in Context and Language to Disagree 🔊 17

Listen to the dialog. Fill in the blanks with the words you hear.

A: I think online shopping is great!

B: Really? How come?

A: Well, I really think online shopping is **economical**. I mean, you can save a lot of money because _____ no clerks and no building. And, you don't have to _____ for transportation.

B: Yeah, but online shopping can be **time-consuming**. I mean, you might spend too much time doing it. Some of my friends spend _____ every week shopping online.

A: Well, some people might do it too _____, but online shopping is **relaxing**. I mean, you can shop comfortably _____ your sofa or bed.

Unit 13

D Controlled Practice Pairwork

Student A looks at this page. Student B looks at page 57. Spend a few minutes filling in the correct adjectives in the blue boxes. Take turns giving opinions about online shopping. Each time you choose an adjective from the box, cross (∕) it off.
Try a few rounds using only blue parts. Then try a few rounds using blue + red parts. To prepare, write only key words (NOT sentences) in the red boxes before you try the dialog.

unsafe	unreliable	time-saving	relaxing
troublesome	practical	economical	time-consuming

Dialog 1

Student A A starts the conversation. Choose the correct adjective to fit the dialog.

Support

1. Have you ever tried online shopping?
3. Really? How come?
5. Yeah, but online shopping is _____. I mean, it saves you a lot of time because
7. But, online shopping is _____. I mean, it's very useful.

Dialog 2

Student A Listen to Student B and choose the correct adjective to fit the dialog.

Support

2. No, not much.
4. Umm, I think online shopping can be _____. I mean, it can be dangerous.
6. Yeah, maybe, but online shopping can be _____. I mean, you can't always trust online shopping.
8. Hmm, ***hold that thought**. I've got to go to the washroom.

* hold that thought. = Just a minute, I have to …
A polite way to stop a discussion (fake excuse)

56

D Controlled Practice Pairwork

Student B looks at this page. Student A looks at page 56. Spend a few minutes filling in the correct adjectives in the blue boxes. Take turns giving opinions about online shopping. Each time you choose an adjective from the box, cross (╱) it off.
Try a few rounds using only blue parts. Then try a few rounds using blue + red parts. To prepare, write only key words (NOT sentences) in the red boxes before you try the dialog.

unsafe	unreliable	time-saving	relaxing
troublesome	practical	economical	time-consuming

Dialog 1

Student B Listen to Student A and choose the correct adjective to fit the dialog.

Support

2. Yeah, once. But, I'm ***not a big fan** of online shopping.
4. Well, I think it can be _____. I mean, you might spend too much time doing it because
6. Yeah, maybe, but online shopping can be _____. I mean, sometimes it's a hassle because
8. Hmm, that's true, but I still prefer shopping in person.

* not a big fan = I don't like it so much
Example: I'm <u>not a big fan</u> of rock music. I <u>don't like</u> rock music <u>so much</u>.

Dialog 2

Student B B starts the conversation. Choose the correct adjective to fit the dialog.

Support

1. Do you do a lot of online shopping?
3. Really? Why not?
5. Well, that's possible, but online shopping is _____. I mean, you can save money.
7. Umm, some sites are unreliable, but online shopping is really _____. I mean, you can shop comfortably.

Unit 14

Students Working Part-Time

Part 1

A Preview Pairwork

1. Read the statements. Check (✓) the information about yourself.

   Me   My Classmate
   ___ ___   I ¹**currently** have a part-time job.
   ___ ___   I work at least 15 hours a week.
   ___ ___   I had a part-time job when I was in high school.
   ___ ___   My hourly ²**wage** at my part-time job is good.
   ___ ___   I like my part-time job.
   ___ ___   I have to work part-time.
   ___ ___   I think all high school students should work part-time.
   ___ ___   I think all college students should have a part-time job.
   ___ ___   I have had more than three different part-time jobs.

   ¹ currently = now   ² wage = pay/salary

2. Change each statement above into a question and interview a classmate. Check (✓) the information about your classmate.

   ### Examples:

   Statement: I currently have a part-time job.
   Question: Do you currently have a part-time job? Where do you work?
   Statement: My hourly wage at my part-time job is good.
   Question: Is the hourly wage at your part-time job good? How much do you make?

   Ask follow-up questions

B Listening

Listen to Ben and Cindy talking about the ideal part-time job. Fill in the blanks with the words you hear.

 18

Cindy: Hey, Ben, what would be the **ideal** part-time job for you? I mean, what would be the _____ part-time job?

Ben: Hmm, that's a good question. I think the ideal part-time job for me would be _____ hours a week, _____ days a week, and an hourly wage of _____ per hour.

Cindy: And, what kind of job would it be? I mean, where would you work?

Ben: Hmm, another good question.

Cindy: I mean, would you work at a convenience store, or a supermarket, or a drugstore? How about a restaurant or _____?

Ben: Hmm, … I think I would work at a fitness center because I like _____.

Cindy: Cool! Maybe it _____ happen.

Q1: What does **ideal** mean? **Ideal** means "_____".

Q2: What does **working out** mean? **Working out** means "_____".

C Interview Pairwork

Ask a classmate about their ideal part-time job.

A: Hey, _____. What would be the ideal part-time job for you?

B: Umm, for me, the ideal part-time job would be _____ hours a week, _____ days a week, and an hourly wage of _____ per hour.

A: And, what kind of job would it be? I mean, where would you work?

B: Umm, I would work at _____ because … .

Unit 14

D **Vocabulary** Choose the correct adjective to match its definition (meaning). Write it in the space. Add *two of your own* adjectives. *Add the meanings of the two new adjectives.*

distracting	vital	valuable	educational	_____
tiresome	time-consuming	stressful	stimulating	_____

1. I think working part-time is _____. I mean, you can learn a lot.
2. I think working part-time is _____. I mean, we need to do it.
3. I think working part-time could be _____. I mean, it could be interesting.
4. I think working part-time is _____. I mean, there are a lot of benefits.
5. I think working part-time could be _____. I mean, you might lose focus.
6. I think working part-time could be _____. I mean, it might be boring.
7. I think working part-time could be _____. I mean, it might take up a lot of your time.
8. I think working part-time could be _____. I mean, it might make you stressed out.
9. I think working part-time could be _____.
   I mean, _____.
10. I think working part-time could be _____.
    I mean, _____.

E **Vocabulary – Expanded** Circle (◯) the word or expression in each group that is not directly connected to the meaning of the adjective (in red or in blue).

Group 1	valuable	useful	rewarding	(spacious)
Group 2	vital	basic	crucial	necessary
Group 3	distracting	destroy	pay too much attention	lose concentration
Group 4	tiresome	tedious	suitable	dull
Group 5	educational	instructive	a learning experience	connecting
Group 6	stressful	worrying	upsetting	painful
Group 7	stimulating	comfortable	motivating	interesting
Group 8	time-consuming	long	lengthy	practical

F Speaking – Discussing the Pros of Working Part-Time `Pairwork`

Practice the conversation with a partner. Student A chooses a Pro Adjective from the box and gives the meaning. Change roles and practice with a new adjective giving the meaning.

Pro Adjectives
valuable   stimulating
vital   educational

— Language Key —
Red Words are hesitation markers. Use them when you need a little time to think before speaking.
Blue words are words you can use to show disagreement.
Underlined words are the meanings of the adjectives.

A: What do you think about working part-time? I mean, do you think it's good?
B: Hmm, I'm not sure. What do you think?
A: Umm, I think it has some good points.
B: Really? Like what?
A: Well, for instance, it's valuable. I mean, there are a lot of benefits.
B: Hmm, I think it depends on the job.

G Speaking – Discussing the Cons of Working Part-Time `Pairwork`

Practice the conversation with a partner. Student A chooses a Con Adjective from the box and gives the meaning. Change roles and practice with a new adjective giving the meaning.

Con Adjectives
time-consuming   tiresome
stressful   distracting

— Language Key —
Red Words are hesitation markers. Use them when you need a little time to think before speaking.
Blue words are words you can use to show disagreement.
Underlined words are the meanings of the adjectives.

A: What do you think about working part-time? I mean, do you think it's good?
B: Hmm, I'm not sure. What do you think?
A: Umm, I think it has some drawbacks.
B: Really? Such as?
A: Well, for one thing, I think it could be tiresome. I mean, it might be boring.
B: Hmm, ... that's true, but it also has some good points.

Unit 15 Students Working Part-Time Part 2

A Building Support   Pairwork

1. Look at the dialog below. Give answers for B's part from your own experience if possible. Then, practice the dialog with a partner. Student A should try to expand the conversation with **follow-up** questions.

B: I **need** the money **for** public transportation.
A: How do you get to school? (Follow-up Q1)
B: Umm, I take the subway and two buses.
A: How long does it take you to get to school? (Follow-up Q2)
B: Umm, about an hour and a half.

A: Do you like working part-time?

B: Yeah, I do.

A: How come?

B: Well, **it's a good way to** earn money.

A: What do you **need** the money **for**?

B: Umm, I **need** the money **for** _____.

   I also **need** the money **for** _____.

school fees (tuition)
living expenses
entertainment
_____

2. Look at the dialog below. Give answers for B's part from your own experience if possible. Then, practice the dialog with a partner.

A: Do you like working part-time?

B: Yeah, I do.

A: How come?

B: Well, **it's a good way to** learn new skills. For example, **I've learned how to**

   1) _____

   2) _____

   How about you? Have you learned any new skills working part-time?

A: Yeah, I've **learned how to**

   1) _____

   2) _____

manage my time
deal with customers
be responsible
use a cash register
make pizzas
_____

Students Working Part-Time Part 2

B Adding Support to the Adjective and Meaning

Match the *Adjective* with its *Meaning* and *Supporting* parts. Check your answers with a partner. Number 1 has been done for you.

Note: Some of the *Adjectives* have **more than one** *Supporting* part!

Adjective	Meaning	Support	
I think working part-time is vital. 1	I mean, it might be boring.	A part-time job is important experience we need before working full-time after graduation. 1,	A part-time job is necessary for making future contacts. 1,
I think working part-time could be stimulating. 2	I mean, it might take up a lot of your time.	Some jobs are dull because you just do the same thing. For example, I just say hello to customers.	It's a good way to earn money for school tuition and other things.
I think working part-time could be tiresome. 3	I mean, we need to do it. 1	For example, it's a good way to learn new skills. You can learn how to manage your time.	I work as a tutor and it's always interesting teaching younger kids.
I think working part-time is valuable. 4	I mean, it could be interesting.	You have to work, go to school, and do homework.	My boss is always yelling at me. And, some customers are rude.
I think working part-time could be time-consuming. 5	I mean, there are a lot of benefits.	I learned how to make Chinese food at the restaurant where I worked.	Some students work around 20 hours a week. That's a lot.
I think working part-time is educational. 6	I mean, it might make you stressed out.	You have to talk to your co-workers and customers.	You might focus too much on your job and not do your school work. You might get poor grades.
I think working part-time could be stressful. 7	I mean, you might lose focus.		
I think working part-time could be distracting. 8	I mean, you can learn a lot.		

C More Support `Pairwork`

Work with a partner and try to answer the questions.

1. Which jobs on this list could be **stimulating**? Circle (○) them. Why are they **stimulating**?

   > office clerk / IT assistant / call center operator / tutor / waitress /
   > convenience store clerk / elderly care home helper / translator

2. What part-time jobs could be **tiresome**? Why? Is your part-time job **tiresome**?
   _____.

3. Why are some part-time jobs **stressful**? Is your part-time job **stressful**? Why?
   _____.

Unit 15

D Controlled Practice Pairwork

Student A looks at this page. Student B looks at page 65. Spend a few minutes filling in the correct adjectives in the blue boxes. Take turns giving opinions about working part-time. Each time you choose an adjective from the box, cross (╱) it off.

Try a few rounds using only blue parts. Then try a few rounds using blue + red parts. To prepare, write only key words (NOT sentences) in the red boxes before you try the dialog.

valuable	distracting	educational	time-consuming
stimulating	tiresome	vital	stressful

Dialog 1

Student A A starts the conversation. Choose the correct adjective to fit the dialog.

Support

1. I really think you should get a part-time job.
3. Well, for one thing, a part-time job is _____. I mean, there are a lot of benefits.
5. Well, a part-time job could be distracting, but a part-time job is _____. I mean, we need to do it because
7. Hmm, ... you have some good points.

Dialog 2

Student A Listen to Student B and choose the correct adjective to fit the dialog.

Support

2. Really? Why?
4. Yeah, but, but a part-time job could also be _____. I mean, it could take up a lot of your time.
6. Yeah, maybe, but a part-time job could be _____. I mean, it could make you stressed out.
8. Yeah, you too. I guess it depends on the job.

D Controlled Practice Pairwork

Student B looks at this page. Student A looks at page 64. Spend a few minutes filling in the correct adjectives in the blue boxes. Take turns giving opinions about working part-time. Each time you choose an adjective from the box, cross (/) it off.

Try a few rounds using only blue parts. Then try a few rounds using blue + red parts. To prepare, write only key words (NOT sentences) in the red boxes before you try the dialog.

valuable	distracting	educational	time-consuming
stimulating	tiresome	vital	stressful

Dialog 1

Student B Listen to Student A and choose the correct adjective to fit the dialog.

Support

2. Really? Why?
4. Yeah, but a part-time job could be _____. I mean, you might lose focus.
6. Yeah, maybe, but a part-time job could also be _____. I mean, it could be boring.
8. You have some good points, too. Maybe I'll think about it.

Dialog 2

Student B B starts the conversation. Choose the correct adjective to fit the dialog.

Support

1. I really think you should get a part-time job.
3. Well, a part-time job is _____. I mean, you can learn a lot.
5. Hmm, that's possible, but I think a part-time job can be _____. I mean, it could be interesting.
7. Hmm, ... You have some good points.

Icon Image Credits: p. 35
©solomon7/Shutterstock.com, ©Artseen/Shutterstock.com, ©Rose Carson/Shutterstock.com

著作権法上、無断複写・複製は禁じられています。

Coffee Shop Discussions - The Foundations of "Good" Discussion　　［B-891］
英語で発信力を鍛えるディスカッション ―日常トピックスで考えを伝えてみよう！―

第1刷	2019年4月1日
第3刷	2024年3月29日
著　者	ボゼア・アラン　Alan Bossaer

| 発行者 | 南雲　一範　Kazunori Nagumo |
| 発行所 | 株式会社　南雲堂 |

〒162-0801　東京都新宿区山吹町361
NAN'UN-DO Co., Ltd.
361 Yamabuki-cho, Shinjuku-ku, Tokyo 162-0801, Japan
振替口座：00160-0-46863
TEL：03-3268-2311（営業部：学校関係）
　　　03-3268-2384（営業部：書店関係）
　　　03-3268-2387（編集部）
FAX：03-3269-2486

| 編集者 | 丸小　雅臣／伊藤　宏実 |

組　版	柴崎　利恵
装　丁	NONdesign
検　印　省　略	
コード	ISBN978-4-523-17891-0　　C0082

Printed in Japan

E-mail : nanundo@post.email.ne.jp
URL : https://www.nanun-do.co.jp/